Wild Britain

Badger

Louise and Richard Spilsbury

H www.heinemann.co.uk
Visit our website to find out more information about **Heinemann Library** books.

To order:
☎ Phone 44 (0) 1865 888066
▤ Send a fax to 44 (0) 1865 314091
▯ Visit the Heinemann Bookshop at www.heinemann.co.uk to browse our catalogue and order online.

First published in Great Britain by Heinemann Library, Halley Court, Jordan Hill, Oxford OX2 8EJ, part of Harcourt Education Ltd. Heinemann is a registered trademark of Harcourt Education Ltd.

Editorial: Lucy Thunder and Helen Cox
Design: David Poole and Celia Floyd
Illustrations: Jeff Edwards, Alan Fraser and Geoff Ward
Picture Research: Catherine Bevan and Maria Joannou
Production: Séverine Ribierre

Originated by Dot Gradations
Printed and bound in Hong Kong, China by South China Printing

ISBN 0 431 03928 3 (hardback)
07 06 05 04 03
10 9 8 7 6 5 4 3 2 1

ISBN 0 431 03935 6 (paperback)
08 07 06 05 04
10 9 8 7 6 5 4 3 2 1

British Library Cataloguing in Publication Data
Spilsbury, Louise and Spilsbury, Richard
Badger. – (Wild Britain)
599.7'67'0941
A full catalogue record for this book is available from the British Library.

Acknowledgements

The Publishers would like to thank the following for permission to reproduce photographs:

Ecoscene pp11, **17**, **22** (Robin Redfern); FLPA p**5** (Hugh Clark), **6** (Derek Middleton), **10**, **19**, **20** (Martin Withers); Nature Photographers p12 (Hugh Clark); NHPA pp**8**, **25**, **29** (Andy Rouse); Oxford Scientific Films pp**4**, **15** (Mark Hamblin), **18**, **23** (Robin Redfern); RSPCA pp**9** (E G Coleman), **13** (James Flynn), **14** (John Howard), **16** (William S Paton), **21** (Colin Seddon), **24** (Ron Perkins), **26** (Mark Hamblin), **27**, **28** (Vanessa Latford).

Cover photograph of a badger, reproduced with permission of Bruce Coleman Collection (Hans Reinhard).

The Publishers would like to thank Michael Scott for his assistance in the preparation of this book.

Every effort has been made to contact copyright holders of any material reproduced in this book. Any omissions will be rectified in subsequent printings if notice is given to the Publishers.

Contents

Any words appearing in the text in bold, **like this**, are explained in the Glossary.

What are badgers?

An adult badger is usually about 90 centimetres long and weighs around 10 kilograms.

Badgers are very easy to recognize. They are large **mammals** with a black and white striped face. They have grey fur on their body and black fur on their legs.

Badgers got their name because of the special 'badge', or markings, on their face.

Male and **female** badgers look alike, but males are slightly bigger. Male badgers are called **boars** and female badgers are called **sows**.

Where badgers live

Over half of the badgers in Britain live in woodlands.

A habitat is a place where wild animals live. Most badgers live in woodland or hedgerow habitats. They also live on sea cliffs, **moorland** and sometimes in fields.

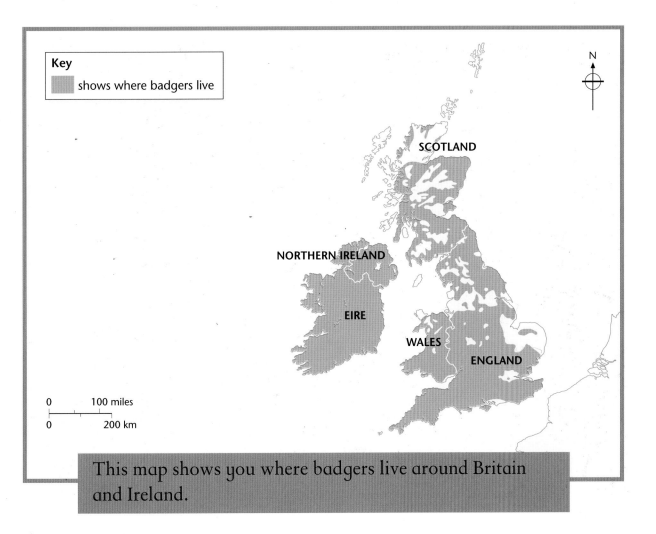

Key

shows where badgers live

SCOTLAND

NORTHERN IRELAND

EIRE

WALES

ENGLAND

N

| 0 | | 100 miles |
| 0 | | 200 km |

This map shows you where badgers live around Britain and Ireland.

Badgers live in almost every part of Britain. They live where there is food to eat and bushes and trees to hide among. Badgers like quiet places away from people.

7

What badgers eat

Badgers eat food that they find or catch on the ground.

Badgers are **omnivores**. They eat parts of plants and small animals. Earthworms are a badger's favourite food – a badger can eat 200 in a night!

This badger is eating an egg it stole from a bird's nest on the ground.

Badgers eat worms, voles, birds, eggs, snails, hedgehogs, **insects**, grass and **roots**. They also eat nuts, seeds and berries that fall to the ground from trees.

Finding food

Badgers usually come out to find food in the early evening.

Badgers are **nocturnal** animals. This means they move around and hunt for food during the night.

Badgers use their long claws to dig up food. They smell or hear things moving below the ground.

Badgers do not have very good eyesight. They find food in the dark using their **sense** of smell. They also have good hearing – they can hear small animals moving around.

On the move

Badgers have a waddling kind of walk. As they go, their rear swings from side to side.

Badgers walk on all four legs. They usually scuffle along with their head down. They often stop to listen for danger or sounds from animals. Sounds can mean that food is near.

Badgers travel up to 6 kilometres a night hunting for food.

Badgers usually travel the same way each time they go out to find food. They make paths through the grass. They can run quite quickly if something frightens them.

Badger setts

The entrance holes to a sett are often near the bottom of a tree.

During the day, badgers rest under ground in homes called **setts**. They dig out setts with the claws on their front legs.

A badger's sett has several entrance holes.

Making scratch marks tells others that this patch is taken.
It is like putting a name or number on your front door!

Badgers often mark the area around their sett by scratching tree trunks. They scratch the trees with their long claws. This tells other badgers to keep away.

Inside a sett

Badgers fill their bedrooms with leaves, moss and grass. This makes soft beds to sleep on.

Badgers dig out long tunnels inside their **sett**. The tunnels lead to rooms deep under the ground. Some rooms are for sleeping and others are to have **cubs** in.

Badgers often carry their bedding outside to freshen it up in the air. Then they take it back down again.

Badgers are clean animals. They often take out old bedding material and change it for fresh grass. They dig holes away from the sett to use as toilets.

Badger groups

A clan is usually made up of several adult badgers and their young.

Some badgers live alone, but most live together in groups. A badger group is called a **clan**.

There may be up to fifteen badgers in a clan.

Each clan stays in a particular **territory**. This is the area they live in and travel around. They know the area very well so they know the best places to find food.

Badger young

Newborn badger cubs are small and helpless. Their mother has to feed and care for them.

Female badgers give birth to **cubs** in a room deep inside their **sett**. A female has two or three cubs in late winter. The cubs spend the first eight weeks inside the sett.

These small cubs are suckling from their mother in the sett.

The cubs feed by **suckling** milk from their mother. Cubs start to go outside the sett with their mother after about eight weeks.

Growing up

The mother badger takes the cubs out and shows them what food to find and eat.

At about eight weeks old a mother badger begins to feed her **cubs** some adult food. Until cubs can catch their own food, mother badgers chew up worms and pass them into a cub's mouth.

Badger cubs chase and play-fight with other cubs.

Cubs spend a lot of time chasing and playing. This helps them to get stronger and quicker. After about one year, young **males** leave the **clan**. **Females** usually stay.

Sounds and smells

This badger is calling out to tell others that danger is near.

Badgers make different sounds to tell each other things. **Cubs** squeal if they are scared. A **boar** growls to scare other badgers away. **Sows** purr when their cubs are near.

When two badgers meet, they smell each other. This helps them find out if they are from the same clan.

Badgers from the same **clan** lick each other a lot. This is called **grooming**. Grooming gives all the badgers in a clan the same smell. This helps them recognize their friends!

Dangers

Buzzards, like this, sometimes catch young badger cubs.

Many badger **cubs** die in cold winters. Foxes catch and eat some cubs. Adult badgers are too big for most hunting animals to catch. They live for up to fourteen years.

Many badgers are injured or killed by cars each year.

In Britain, many badgers are killed by cars when they try to cross a road. Some badger **setts** are destroyed when people clear land to build new roads or houses.

A badger's year

Cubs start to find their own food in spring, when there are lots of earthworms for them to eat.

Cubs are born early in the year. They come out of the **sett** in spring. They need to feed and grow a lot to store fat for the cold winter.

Badgers take lots of grass and straw into the sett for winter sleeps.

In winter, it is cold and there is less food. Badgers sleep for several days at a time. They live on fat they stored earlier. They also go out to feed every few days.

Animal groups

Scientists group together animals that are alike. Badgers are in the same group as stoats and otters. They are all short-legged **mammals**, with claws and sharp teeth.

badger

stoat

otter

The artwork on this page is not to scale.

Glossary

boar   male badger

clan   group of badgers that live together

cub   baby badger

female   animal which can become a mother when it is grown up. A female human is called a woman or a girl.

grooming   when animals lick and clean each other

insect   small animal that has six legs when an adult. Bees, wasps and beetles are insects.

male   animal which can become a father when it is grown up. A male human is called a man or a boy.

mammals   group of animals that includes humans. All mammals feed their babies their own milk and have some hair on their bodies.

moorland   cool windy area on a hill, covered by grasses and heather

nocturnal   active at night and resting during the day

omnivore   animal that eats parts of plants and other animals for food

roots   parts of a plant that grow below the ground

scientist   person who studies the world around us and the things in it to find out how they work

senses   most animals have five senses – sight, hearing, touch, taste and smell

sett   underground home of a group of badgers

sow   female badger

suckle   when a mother feeds her baby with milk from her body

territory   area of land where an animal lives and feeds

Index